THE LYRICAL POEMS
VON HOFMANNSTHAL

Translated from the German with an Introduction
by Charles Wharton Stork

NEW HAVEN · YALE UNIVERSITY PRESS
LONDON · HUMPHREY MILFORD
OXFORD UNIVERSITY PRESS · MDCCCCXVIII

To My Friend

ERIC R. D. MACLAGAN

Who Introduced Me to the Poetry of
Hofmannsthal

Preface and Acknowledgments

The present volume of translations comprises all the contents of Hofmannsthal's *Die Gesammelte Gedichte,* Insel Verlag, Leipsic, 1907 (in my edition), with the exception of *Der Tod des Tizian,* a play. This play, with *Tor und Tod,* has been translated for *The German Classics,* vol. XVII, by Mr. John Heard, Jr., who has also done the prologue on the death of Böcklin here included. Another version of *Tor und Tod* by Elisabeth Walter has appeared with The Gorham Press. *Die Hochzeit der Sobeide,* a longer play, has been done for the Classics, vol. XX, by Professor Bayard Quincy Morgan. Hofmannsthal's most famous play, *Elektra,* translated by Arthur Symons, has been brought out by Brentano.

Of the poems here included, the *Ballade of the Outward Life* has been translated by Margarete Münsterberg in her *Harvest of German Verse,* Appleton. In *German Lyrists of To-day* by Daisy Broicher, Elkin Mathews, London, appear *Early Spring, Thy Face* and *The Two.* An article by Elisabeth Walter, entitled *Hugo von Hofmannsthal, an Exponent of Modern Lyricism,* in *The Colonnade* magazine for December, 1916, New York, contains again the *Ballade of the Outward Life* and *The Two* with the third of the *Three Little Songs* and a number of fragments.

Of my own translations *Of Mutability, Travel Song* and *Interdependence* appeared in *The German Classics,* vol. XVII, and are here republished by the courtesy of the proprietors, the German Publication Society. The Introduction has been greatly expanded from an article in the New York *Nation* which contained translations of *The Two, A Dream of the Higher Magic* and the third of the *Three Little Songs.* They are reproduced here by the courtesy of the proprietors of *The Nation.* Several other poems, accepted by *Poet Lore,* are included by the kind permission of the publishers. The entire volume is brought out by the kind permission of Herr von Hofmannsthal through his publishers, the Insel Verlag, Leipsic

These translations aim at being as true to the spirit, more particularly the mood, of the originals as possible. They are fairly literal, the changes being mainly in the order of words in a phrase. Very occasionally whole lines have been transposed. The metres and rhyme-schemes are, with slight exceptions, as nearly identical as possible. As Hofmannsthal's poetry is so notably compressed and full of meaning, it is hoped that these translations, together with the Introduction, may enable some of those who already know him in the original to see even more in his work than they have already done.

CHARLES WHARTON STORK.

"Birdwood," Philadelphia.

CONTENTS

HOFMANNSTHAL AS A LYRIC POET

The name of Hugo von Hofmannsthal is fairly well known to those who attempt to follow the course of modern literature in Europe. Furthermore, all opera-goers have come in contact with it from the accident that two of Hofmannsthal's plays, *Elektra* and *Der Rosenkavalier*, were set to music by Richard Strauss. His *Elektra* was also acted in New York by Mrs. Patrick Campbell. It may nevertheless be safely said that the peculiar genius of this author is but little appreciated in America, and that the general impression among those who have heard of him is of a colorful, neoclassical dramatist. It is hoped that the present volume may serve to bring out another and deeper aspect of the poet.

Judged by bulk, the lyrics of Hofmannsthal's might well be neglected in a survey of his writings as a whole. He has to his credit some seven or eight long plays, a dozen short plays and two volumes of prose studies. Against these we can set only a small volume entitled *Die Gesammelte Gedichte*, including, apparently, all the poems which the author cares to have preserved. It contains but twenty-three lyrics, the rest of the book consisting of a short play, a dramatic idyll and several prologues written for special occasions. But as the short plays excel the longer in concentrated art, so the lyrics

1

excel both. Out of this mere handful the most general German anthologies take some three or four poems. In a collection of 536 poems covering a period of 700 years *The Oxford Book of German Verse* includes three examples of Hofmannsthal. *Die Ernte,* a similar anthology, published in Germany, gives him four pages out of 466. This is no mean proportion for a living poet born so late as 1874. Besides, the level of thought and technic is so maintained throughout the small body of lyrics that (with one exception) the critic is hard put to it to decide which are the best. An entire school of younger poets is imitating Hofmannsthal, as art students may be seen copying the few authentic Giorgiones, Bellinis or Vermeers.

I

But despite Hofmannsthal's high reputation in his own literature, we may as well admit at once that his poetry is confined to a field of interest far removed from the thoughts of the average American. We can hardly come into a receptive state of mind toward him without picturing to ourselves the environment which shaped his genius.

The outward events of Hofmannsthal's life appear surprisingly normal. He was born in Vienna February 1, 1874, received the usual broad education of the cultivated Austrian, traveled, married, and settled at Rodaun, a quiet suburb of the capital. Up to the time of the war he was living the life of a secluded literary man with his wife and chil-

2

dren, sometimes gracing a special event in the city and occasionally making an excursion to visit his friends in Paris or Italy.

It is to Hofmannsthal's environment in Vienna that the peculiar trend of his art may be traced. There was perhaps no city twenty-five years ago where a young man of means and birth could live a life so completely detached from that of his modern fellow-men. The repose of antiquity was preserved there more completely even than in Paris; there was little intrusion of the Nineteenth Century business world on the traditions of Maria Theresa's court, little ferment of democratic ideals of any kind. Beautiful gardens, Romanesque churches, palaces contemporary with Versailles, galleries rich in Italian masterpieces—these were the elements that surrounded the minds of young men. Social and political questions were put to one side or cheerfully left to those whose concern they were supposed to be. Certain conditions were admitted to be hopelessly bad, and, if so, why should one trouble oneself about them? Grace and gaiety were the prevailing characteristics of Viennese life, as of its typical expression, the Viennese waltz.

To the young man who was able to indulge his taste art was the chief end and purpose of being. Goethe had already set the example of artistic aloofness by retiring to his study to write the *West-Östliche Divan,* while the battles of the Napoleonic Wars were being fought around him. The connect-

3

ing link between Goethe and the Vienna of the Nineties was the tradition of Franz Grillparzer, Austria's great neo-classical dramatist, who died in 1872. As Goethe introduced modern characterization into the story of Iphigenia, Grillparzer followed with his plays on Hero and Leander, Sappho, and Medea. Other dramatists, such as Raimund and Wilbrandt, carried on the tendency of cultivating a drama far removed from the existence of those who witnessed it, the subjects being sometimes classical, sometimes fanciful, sometimes from mediæval history. The influence of Shakespeare was turned in the same direction: namely, toward one or another phase of romanticism. Beauty of proportion, delicate fancy, and nobility of sentiment were the chief requirements of the drama, the most brilliant field of literary activity in Vienna. Italy, the ideal home of romance, was easily accessible. Painters, with a few notable exceptions, turned their faces thitherward. Music and the ballet, always prominent in the Austrian capital, are by their very nature detached from realism. Thus the cultivated man of Vienna was almost by compulsion an æsthete.

Grillparzer* thought the North Germans had cultivated their understanding at the expense of their feeling, and had thereby impaired their æsthetic sense. But though the typical Austrian is "a man of

* Quoted from the life of Grillparzer by Professor W. G. Howard, *German Classics*, vol. VI, p. 233.

feeling," the human mind everywhere must, it seems, have problems to solve. If the contemporary world be shut out, these problems will naturally be subjective. Also, as many observers have noted, listening to sweet music and looking on at a scene of continued gaiety are apt to induce a pleasurable, but often profound, mood of melancholy. The sojourner in Italy, particularly in Venice, may have been struck with a similar feeling.

II

We may seem to have wandered rather far afield, but as a matter of fact I have tried, in the preceding part of this introduction, to write the biography of Hugo von Hofmannsthal in the only way that came to hand. There is no poem translated in this volume which will not be largely accounted for by the considerations that have just been presented. Instead of being a unique and totally unrelated personality in literature, Hofmannsthal was in many respects the normal product of these, to us, abnormal conditions.

He had, however, a marked personality in addition. In the first place he may be called an extremist of his kind: an extreme lover of rich and remote beauty, an artist unusually detached from everyday existence, a genius of oppressive melancholy, a magician of startling power in the revelation of human consciousness, an unequaled exponent of style. Furthermore, all these faculties appeared in

5

him at so early an age as to make him a literary prodigy, in this respect (as in others to be noted later) resembling Rossetti. In his first short plays, *Gestern* and *Tod des Tizian*, written at the ages of seventeen and eighteen respectively, his style was already that of a mature master. He has since exhibited greater variety, but hardly greater power. As a boy of seventeen Hofmannsthal was acclaimed by many critics as technically the greatest German poet since Goethe.

The bent of Hofmannsthal's genius soon brought him into association with two similarly minded German poets: Stefan George and Rainer Maria Rilke. These three united in a publication called *Blätter für die Kunst* to combat the unmitigated realism of contemporary German literature, as represented by the plays of Sudermann and the poetry of Liliencron. The three young apostles of beauty maintained that* "the poet, in order to depict life as life really is, must take no part in it." Of George's work Hofmannsthal wrote in words that may equally be applied to himself:† "He so completely conquered life, so absolutely mastered it, that from his poems the rare, indescribable peace and refreshing coolness of a still, dark temple are wafted upon our noise-racked senses."

But Hofmannsthal did not, like his associates,

* Quoted by permission from an article on Hofmannsthal by Elisabeth Walter in the *Colonnade,* December, 1916, New York.
† Ibid.

leave his fame to rest on lyric poetry. He went on
for a time with the one-act poetical soul-dramas of
which *Gestern* was the first. Of these the finest
and best known are *Tor und Tod, Der Weisse
Fächer* and *Die Frau im Fenster,* all deeply imagi-
native studies of great spiritual moments. The
third, which (though almost entirely a monologue)
is the most dramatic of the three, has been acted in
New York. Then came longer plays on original
themes, the best of which is *Die Hochzeit der
Sobeide.*

Hofmannsthal's greatest success, however, has
been won with plays which, like Goethe's *Iphigenie*
and Grillparzer's *Medea,* are modeled around
themes of earlier dramatic masterpieces. His
method is simply to take the old story, rearrange
the scenes freely, and completely re-create the char-
acters. In the case of his best-known play *Elektra*
he does but do as Euripides did: namely, render
the dignified characters of the earlier Greek trage-
dians thoroughly human from the standpoint of a
later day. Thus the treatment of Elektra in Hof-
mannsthal's play has been called pathological, be-
cause that is the only way in which, with our
demand for psychology, we can be made to realize
the state of the human mind in so terrible a situa-
tion. The effect is certainly "unclassic" and to
many people too painfully human. But on any
score *Elektra* is an important play. Hofmannsthal
has given a similarly free rendering of classic ma-

7

terial in *Ödipus und die Sphinx* and has also translated Sophocles' play as *König Ödipus*.

The influence of the English drama appears in a recasting of Otway's *Venice Preserved* as *Das Gerettete Venedig,* in which far greater verisimilitude is given to the characters than was the fashion in Otway's time. Hofmannsthal has also handled very freely the theme of the old morality *Everyman,* giving a skilful German coloring by infusing material from an old play of Hans Sachs. In his last plays, *Christinas Heimreise* and *Der Rosenkavalier,* we find the author successful in his first attempts at comedy. Two volumes of *Prosaische Schriften* consist of subtle studies in literature, in religion, and in character. Among these the essay *Shakespeare's Könige und Grosse Herren* may be noted.

III

With some knowledge of Hofmannsthal's career and literary proclivities, we may proceed to examine the small but very important body of non-dramatic poetry here to be presented. The principle to be kept in mind throughout is, as Miss Walter has well phrased it:* "Every one of Hofmannsthal's poems expresses some condition of the soul in terms of beauty, and always the universal behind the beautiful." The well-worn axiom that beauty is truth has seldom been better exemplified since the time of Keats.

* Cf. the article in the *Colonnade* already cited.

The beauty of Hofmannsthal's poetry should need little further comment, even when his work is given only in translation. Miss Walter cites a criticism on his poems:* "They were not written to instruct, but to arouse sensation, to awaken the indescribable." We must not, however, lose touch with the imaginative truth that underlies these poems, the† "ugly facts" represented in "pretty symbols." That the symbols of Hofmannsthal's poetry are far from being a mere play of fancy, the author indicates in his prologue *For a Similar Book:*

For we have made a play from out the life
We live, and mingled with our comedy
Our truth keeps ever gliding in and out . . .
    etc.

It is in the interfusion of universal truth with beauty of rhythm, with verbal melody, and with colorful imagery that the magic of the poet consists. In any given piece he at once creates the mood appropriate to his central idea, so that the reader, delighted by the art, soon gives up any attempt at cold analysis. The thought is first melted into a feeling such as might be inspired by music, then the feeling is defined by a succession of mental pictures. A typical example of this is found in the poem *A Vision*. The blending of the theme, Death, with the glowing picture and the deep cellolike music of the verse should, unless the translation

* Cf. the article in the *Colonnade* already cited.
† Cf. "Prologue to the Book *Anatol*."

is an utter failure, be easily apparent. But it is perhaps incorrect to speak of blending, where the poem is so entirely an organic unit. Hofmannsthal* deprecates the use of the terms "inward" and "outward" with reference to art and life, because to him they express no real distinction.

Although Hofmannsthal was a product of his environment and was even part of a literary tendency, the forcefulness of his genius was sufficient to raise him far above his possible rivals. Neither the vaguely mystical lyrics of Stefan George nor the wistful reveries of Rilke can compare in ultimate importance with the work of their associate. The intellect of Hofmannsthal dominates the school to which he belongs and has already called forth many followers. He is the one symbolist writing in German who has an absolutely sure touch, a perfect sense of balance in all that he does. In this respect also his plays seem to me to excel those of Maeterlinck.

The English poets who most resemble Hofmannsthal are Vaughan, Blake, Rossetti and Francis Thompson. Vaughan's ability to soar into a world of spiritual exaltation is not unlike what we find in *A Dream of the Higher Magic*. Vaughan, however, takes his moral sense and his human feelings with him, whereas the dæmon of Hofmannsthal surveys all things impersonally. The splendor of their lan-

* Cf. Professor Seiberth's Life of Hofmannsthal, *German Classics,* vol. XVII, p. 484.

10

guage and imagery is very similar, except that the brilliance of the English poet shows in flashes, that of the Austrian in a deep and constant glow. Blake is like Hofmannsthal in the abstractness of his poetic world, and his doctrine that the imagination is God comes very near that pictured in *A Dream of the Higher Magic.* But Blake's expression is simple and intuitive; his is altogether a more aërial spirit.

In their combination of somewhat heavily decorative style with mystic thought, Rossetti and Thompson stand much nearer to Hofmannsthal than do the earlier poets. "Fundamental brainwork," to quote Rossetti's famous phrase, is almost equally evident in the three; the underlying plan of their poems is laid with a similar definiteness. Hofmannsthal differs from Rossetti in that he gives more general pictures, producing effects more purely like those of music; whereas the pre-Raphaelite revels in sharply drawn detail. Both Rossetti and Thompson seem much more passionate; Hofmannsthal's emotion is always subdued and even in texture. The quaint, rather self-conscious style of the two modern English poets contrasts with the smooth diction of Hofmannsthal, whose mind moves in its dim spiritual world with the seemingly unconscious grace of a golden fish in shadowy depths.

IV

Because the quality of Hofmannsthal's mood is so all-pervasive, we have spoken much of the effects which his poetry produces, without giving more than a hint of its actual content. This content might be defined as impersonally subjective, if the phrase does not seem to be an oxymoron. What is meant is that Hofmannsthal writes of his own consciousness, or that of others with whom he for the moment identifies himself, in a manner which shows great power of divination but only the most remote shade of sympathy. He does not wish human emotion to disturb him in his attempt to contemplate reality. For instance, in *The Two* he symbolizes admirably the mysterious relation of sex to sex, but we who read, instead of being stirred to a poignant feeling of pity, are only impelled to murmur: "How strange is truth!" Similarly in the poem *Of Mutability,* when he says it is

A thing too dreadful for the trivial tear:
That all things glide away from out our clasp,

we are in no real danger of a tear or even of a shudder. This impassive attitude toward the facts of life gives a tone of fatalism to nearly every poem in the volume. The interest shown in nature and humanity is exclusively artistic and speculative.

The earlier poems of this volume are purely philosophical or symbolic of the poet's own sensations. The *Three Little Songs* are somewhat more personal than the pieces which precede them; but even the third, a most delicate bit of lyricism, has not the ring of ordinary human feeling. In the

12

remarkable group of *Figures* the poet identifies his soul with those of such various persons as the Emperor of China, a child, a captive ship's cook, and the collective personality of several interacting characters at a social entertainment. Into each of these minds in turn we are made to enter by the same exquisite art which, in the earlier lyrics, enables us to examine the intimacies of the poet's own consciousness. The *Idyll* at the end is a neo-classic study of the same kind, except that, instead of being static, it has dramatic motion, thus pointing the reader on to Hofmannsthal's plays.

We have still to mention the *Prologues and Ad-dresses-of-Mourning*. These, though in a somewhat different vein, are wonderfully fascinating poems. The prologue to *Anatol* is a delicious piece of atmosphere. With the following prologue it constitutes, as we have indicated, a good exposition of the author's artistic purpose: namely, to present the truth, but only under the mask of beauty. In this point Hofmannsthal differs from Arthur Schnitzler, author of the short realistic plays grouped under the title *Anatol*. Schnitzler, though he is what we might call a selective realist, lets us at times see the ugliness of life pretty clearly.

Tributes to the two actors, Mitterwurzer and Müller, show how intensely Hofmannsthal feels the identity of soul and body. He is, to be sure, thinking only of the soul of the given actor, but this soul has the gift of so informing and transforming

13

the body it inhabits that the two cannot be thought of as separate, but only as mingled in varying proportions. The poem on Böcklin is of course the finest of the five, showing as it does how the spirit of a true artist can "adorn the image of the world" for us and can thus live in the added charm which it flings over the visible forms of nature.

V

Professor Seiberth writes:* "As a thinker Hofmannsthal is not in any definite sense a didactic or philosophical poet. The true poet is temperamentally incapable and impatient of close systematic thinking." Without stopping further to confute the absurdity of the second statement than by mentioning the names of Dante, Milton, Shelley and Goethe, we may well examine the validity of the first. A noted† Professor of Philosophy, who is unusually well acquainted with modern literature, says that Hofmannsthal is the greatest living philosophic poet in Europe. This raises a question we can not afford to pass over.

Of course it is possible for many readers not interested in pure philosophy to enjoy Hofmannsthal's poetry simply as poetry, but a little examination will convince most of them that the poet has a remarkably well-defined conception of the universe. In the first place, he "thinks unity" very strongly,

* *German Classics,* vol. XVII, p. 484.
† Prof. Edgar Singer of the University of Pennsylvania.

he feels the deep connection between all times, all places and all things, whether spiritual or material. This is superbly imaged in the lines of *Interdependence:*

> From the weariness of forgotten peoples
> Vainly would I liberate mine eyelids,
> Or would keep my startled soul at distance
> From the silent fall of far-off planets.

But a more unusual doctrine, exemplified in *A Dream of the Higher Magic,* has been taken from the philosophy of Giordano Bruno. Bruno's* hypothesis pictures the soul of man as standing midway between the divine intelligence and the world of what we call external phenomena. It is immortal because it partakes of the divine existence. Its highest function is to contemplate the divine unity which is discoverable in the manifold appearances of material objects. Take now the concluding lines of the poem:

> Our soul's a Cherub, and of lordly birth—
> Dwells not in us, but in some upper star
> Fixes his throne and leaves us oft in dearth.

> Yet deep in us his fiery motions are:
> —So in my dream I seemed to understand—
> And he holds converse with yon fires afar,
> And lives in me as I do in my hand.

* Cf. *Encyclopedia Britannica,* Ninth Edition, sub Bruno.

15

We may here take it that the Adept is none other than man's soul (or, as Blake would have said, imagination), the supposedly eternal power that comes into the human mind and performs all manner of marvels, overleaping the material boundaries of time and space. This "Greatest Magician," or (as he is later called) "Cherub," is the medium of communication between Divinity and Mortality. He may be analyzed after the Hegelian fashion into the antithetical concepts of spirit and matter, with the understanding that these two are in reality indivisibly united. Hofmannsthal has also undertaken in this poem to solve the problems of time and space, and of appearance and reality by assuming all of these to be conditions of our thinking, which therefore the mind, when stimulated by special inspiration, can transcend. From this poem it would seem (Professor Seiberth to the contrary notwithstanding) that Hofmannsthal was in a very definite sense a philosophical poet.

Similar ideas to those just spoken of may be found throughout the poems in this volume. Of course they can not always be so clearly perceived. I can hardly hazard a guess at what is meant by *Life-Song*. *World-Secret* is evidently not meant to convey more than an elusive suggestion. *Such Stuff as Dreams* would seem to express an idea similar to that of *A Dream of the Higher Magic*. Perhaps the child is the link which binds the dream and the moon, as the cherub is the link which binds

16

"yon fires afar" with mortal life. The other poems can, I think, be enjoyed at least as well without the intrusion of any further analysis.

VI

In the spring of 1908 I had the honor of calling on Herr von Hofmannsthal at his house in Rodaun. His way of life appeared extremely simple, there being a notable absence of the paraphernalia of luxury in the rooms I saw. There were none of the pictures or other works of art which a connoisseur of beauty might be supposed to revel in. It has since occurred to me that probably the poet does not care to have his eyes and mind distracted by numerous objects.

Herr von Hofmannsthal is a well-built man of middle height with a high, square forehead, rather sensuous nose and lips, and very dark hair, mustaches and eyes. Without seeming secretive, he managed to reveal almost nothing of himself in our talk, asking me questions most of the time about the old English drama. The only remark he made on himself was when, in answer to some tribute of admiration on his work, he said: "I realize that I write for only about five hundred people in Europe."

Though some of Hofmannsthal's plays have been very successful on the stage and have run to from ten to thirty editions, the fact remains that his best work is for the few. He does not picture life as the ordinary man sees it or can see it. He generalizes what he sees in nature and eliminates the detail, like the designer of a stained-glass window. His interest in a given idea, scene or personality is only for the purpose of arriving at some philosophical conclusion. The result in his art is arresting, both intellectually and æsthetically, but cannot be dissociated in the reader's mind from a feeling of monotony and oppression, as if one were shut up in the darkly beautiful temple to which Hofmannsthal compares the poetry of Stefan George. There is a lack of free air and natural light. His thought has, far more than Matthew Arnold's, the melancholy of the pantheist.

But what a master of imagery! How wonderfully this young poet succeeds in conveying the deep dreams of his imagination! His figures of speech show a particular fondness for children, whose eyes seem to him to behold more of mystery than the power of language can express. He loves the stage, because there the soul can best show its power to transform itself. His outdoor nature is never specified in any particular country, except that the *Travel Song* must refer to Italy, the favorite setting of his early plays. But though certain preferences are apparent in the figures of speech, the memorable power and originality of the Hofmannsthal simile (which is also a symbol) can be explained only by genius.

Imagery can always, in some sort, be translated;

18

verbal felicity must of course be largely lost, or at best but partly re-created, in a new medium of expression. Though Hofmannsthal is so often thought of as a stylist, he has no obtrusive mannerism of form. He obtains large effects by comparatively simple and direct means. Style with him is not a trick, but a gift; the mood clothes itself with the fitting expression, that is all one can say. As the mood is so often somber, the sound of the words is correspondingly sonorous and full of gloomy dignity. In the *Lines to a Little Child,* however, the tone is naïve and gay, in *Society* it is confused and animated. The variety of verse-form is likewise considerable, marked preference being given to the Italian *terza rima,* which is peculiarly suited to the complex, closely woven quality of the thought.

In conclusion, we must concede that Hofmannsthal's lyric poetry is a highly special literary phenomenon. Professor Grummann objects that* "it is pervaded by an artistic atmosphere acquired by idling in art museums rather than in immediate contact with life." To this we may answer that there are two opposite definitions of what is meant by life. It is one thing to describe in the manner of an observant traveler the scenes and persons which meet the outward eye; it is another to reveal the soul to itself. To most persons the second sort of artist will mean very little, but to a few he will give a delight that is almost overpowering. Under the

* *German Classics,* vol. XVIII, pp. 289-290.

spell of Hofmannsthal one feels as when listening to the Andante of a mighty symphony written in a minor key. The poet, like a leader in his orchestral eminence, dominates his audience in soul, mind and body. From such moments we return to the uses of ordinary life in surprise at how deeply we were rapt by the potency of the master's art.

EARLY SPRING.

The spring wind is gliding
  Mid boughs that are bare,
In his heart hiding
  Strange things and rare.

His cradle hath swung
  In sob-shaken air,
And oft hath he clung
  In passion-loosed hair.

Acacia blossoms
  Beneath him snowed,
His breath cooled the bosoms
  That throbbing glowed.

Lips in their laughter
  First he would claim,
Soft fields thereafter
  Woke when he came.

The flute he passed through in
  A sobbing cry,
The sunset's red ruin
  He swiftly flew by.

In silence proceeding
  Through whispering rooms,
And quenched with his speeding
  The lamps' yellow blooms.

23

Early   The spring wind is gliding
Spring   Mid boughs that are bare,
In his heart hiding
    Strange things and rare.

Through the reviving
    Alleys and meadows
His breath is driving
    Wraith-like shadows.

A scent without name
    He bears in his flight
From whence he came
    Since yester-night.

24

A VISION [*Erlebnis*].

The valley with a silver-grayish mist
Of twilight was o'erbrimmed, as when the moon
Filters through clouds.   And yet it was not night.
In the silver-grayish mist of yon dark valley
My twilight-shimmering thoughts were wholly
      blended;
Softly I sank into the shifting depths
Of that transparent sea—and left this life.
What wondrous flowers bloomed about me there
With darkly glowing chalices!—dim thickets
Transfused with streams of reddish-yellow light,
Warm as a glowing topaz.   And the vale
Was filled with deep vibrating harmony
Of melancholy music.   Then I knew—
Though how, I comprehend not—yet I knew
That this was Death; Death was transformed to
      music,
Mightily yearning, sweet, and darkly glowing,
Akin to deepest melancholy.
               Yet—
How strange! a sort of homesickness for life
Wept silently within my soul, it wept
As one may weep when on a towering ship,
That drives toward evening with gigantic sails
Across the dark-blue waves, he passes by
A town, his native town.   He sees before him
The streets, he hears the fountains gush, he breathes
The scent of lilac-bushes; on the bank

25

A Vision He sees himself a child with childish eyes
Anxious and almost weeping, sees a light
Through the wide window burning in his room.
But the huge vessel bears him ever on,
Silently speeding o'er the dark-blue waves
With giant sails of yellow, strangely shaped.

TRAVEL SONG.

Water plunges to devour us,
Rocks would crush with rolling leap,
Strong-winged birds to overpower us
Haunt our path with threatening sweep.

But beneath us lies a land
Where, in ageless lakes reflected,
Ripened fruits forever glow.
Marble fount and statue stand
Deep in groves of bloom protected,
And the gentle breezes blow.

THE TWO.

Her hand bore well the cup to him—
—Her cheek and mouth were like its rim—
So lightly, surely, too, she stepped
That not a drop the rim o'erlept.

As light and firm too was *his* hand;
His fiery mount but fresh from pasture
At one impulsive, easy gesture
Stood quivering where he bade it stand.

Yet it befell that when his hand
Would take from hers the drink unwasted,
The feat for both was overmuch;
For both so trembled at the touch,
That fingers failed, and on the sand
The precious wine rolled down untasted.

LIFE–SONG.

On peacock, lamb and eagle
His youthful lordship brave
May waste the ointment regal
An old dead woman gave.
The dead, whose flight upstreameth
And o'er the tree-tops gleameth,—
Naught more are these, he deemeth,
Than dancers' robes that wave.

He goes as if no justling
Behind e'er threateneth.
He smiles whene'er the rustling
Of Life's robe whispers: Death!
For every place delights him
And every door invites him,
Each passion-wave incites him
As lone he wandereth.

When wild-bee swarms are winging,
His soul pursues in play;
The dolphins with their singing
Upbear him on his way.
All countries are his dwelling,
But soon with hand compelling
A dark stream, ever swelling,
Will bound his shepherd's-day.

.   .   .

On peacock, lamb and eagle
My lord with laughter brave

29

Life-Song May waste the ointment regal
An old dead woman gave,
On friends a smile bestowing,
Through Life's fair garden going
Toward dim gulfs, all unknowing,
From which no skill can save.

"THY FACE. . . ."   *"Thy Face"*

Thy face was laden all with reverie.
Silent and trembling then I looked on thee.
Ah how the thought came back! that even so
Upon a former night I yielded me

Unto the moon and that belovèd vale
Where on the naked hill-side rose a frail
And broken screen of pines, around whose stems
Low-flying cloudlets oftentimes would sail,

While freshly, strangely through the stillness clave
The dashing of the pallid silvery wave
From the deep river,—How it all came back!—
How it came back! For to those things I gave

My very soul in mighty yearning there,
Yea, to that scene, so fruitless and so fair;
As now I yield me to thine eyes that glow,
And to the magic of thy loosened hair.

31

WORLD–SECRET.

The deep well knows it certainly;
Once all things else were deep and still,
And all then knew their fill

Like master-words a child lisps o'er,
From mouth to mouth the tale doth flit
And no one comprehendeth it.

The deep well knows it certainly;
And leaning there a man would know,
But rising up, would lose it so,

Would wildly talk, and make a song.—
O'er this dark mirror, as it chanced,
A child leant down and was entranced.

And grew, and knew itself no more,
And was a woman; then love came
And—who the gifts of love can name,

And all the knowledge love bestows?—
In kisses was she deeply ware
Of dim-divinèd memories rare. . . .

Within our words it lieth hid,
As beggars' feet o'er sand might pace
Above a jewel's resting-place.

The deep well knows it certainly;
Once in this lore were all men wise,
Now but a vague dream, circling, flies.

32

OF THE OUTWARD LIFE [*Ballade des Outward*
Ausseren Lebens].   *Life*

And children, that with deep unknowing gaze
Look out upon the world, grow up and die,
And all men travel on their several ways.

And sweet fruits after bitter follow nigh,
Till like dead birds by night they fall to ground
And in few days wax rotten where they lie.

And still the wind blows, and we hear the sound
Of words and utter them with idle breath,
And joy we feel and weariness profound.

And roads there are where one encountereth
Cities, with trees and lights in glittering range;
Some threatening, some withered as in death. . . .

Why are these built, each to the other strange
In form and fashion, though no few they be?
And why do tears and laughter interchange?

What are these childish toys to us, since we
Are full-grown men, who live apart each one
And roam without a goal unceasingly?

What boots it much to have seen the while we
        roam?—
And yet he sayeth much, who "Evening" saith.
A word whence deep and solemn meanings run

Like heavy honey from the hollow comb.

33

Mutability OF MUTABILITY [*Terzinen I*].

Still, still upon my cheek I feel their breath:
How can it be that days which seem so near
Are gone, forever gone, and lost in death?

This is a thing that none may rightly grasp,
A thing too dreadful for the trivial tear:
That all things glide away from out our clasp;—

And that this I, unchecked by years, has come
Across into me from a little child,
Like an uncanny creature, strangely dumb;—

That I existed centuries past—somewhere,
That ancestors on whom the earth is piled
Are yet as close to me as my very hair,

As much a part of me as my very hair.

34

DEATH [*Terzinen II*].   *Death*

What hours are those! when, shiningly outspread,
The ocean lures us, and we lightly learn
The solemn lore of death, and feel no dread:

As little girls, whose great eyes seem to yearn,
Girls that have pallid cheeks and limbs a-cold,
Some evening look far out and do not turn

Their feebly-smiling gaze, for, loosing hold
Upon their slumber-drunken limbs, the flood
Of life glides over into grass and wold;—

Or as a saint pours out her martyr blood.

"Such Stuff as Dreams" "SUCH STUFF AS DREAMS" [*Terzinen III*].

Such stuff as dreaming is we mortals be,
And every dream doth open wide its eyes
Like a small child beneath a cherry tree,

Above whose top across the deepening skies
The pale full-moon emerges for its flight.—
Not otherwise than so our dreams arise.

They live as a child that laughs, and to the sight
Appear no smaller on their curving way
Than the full-moon awakening on the night.

Our inmost self is open to their sway,
As spirit hands in sealèd chambers gleam
They dwell in us and have their life alway.

And three are one: the man, the thing, the dream.

36

INTERDEPENDENCE [*Manche Freilich . . .*]. *Inter-*

Many men no doubt must die below-decks
Where the heavy oars of the ship are plying;
Others dwell above beside the tiller
Know the flight of birds and the lore of star-lands.

Many with weighted limbs must lie forever
At the roots of the labyrinthine life-tree;
Others have their place appointed
With the sibyls, the queens of vision,
Where they bide as in seats accustomed,
Head untroubled and hand unburdened.

Yet from yonder lives a shadow falleth
On the happier lives of the others,
And the light unto the heavy
As to air and earth are fettered:

From the weariness of forgotten peoples
Vainly would I liberate mine eyelids,
Or would keep my startled soul at distance
From the silent fall of far-off planets.

Many fates with mine are interwoven,
Subtly mingled flow the threads of being,
And my share in it is more than merely
One life's narrow flame or thin-toned lyre.

37

A DREAM OF THE HIGHER MAGIC.

Far kinglier than a chain of pearls both seem,
And bold as morning-misted ocean blue,
Such—as methought then—was the mighty dream.

The doors of glass were wide, the wind went
        through.—
In a pavilion close to earth I slept,
And through four open doors the breezes flew.—

And first a troop of bridled horses swept
Before my bed, and hounds too in a pack.
But with a sudden gesture the Adept—

That Greatest, First Magician—drew me back
Unto a wall, between the which and me
Swayed his proud head, the long hair kingly black.

And straight no wall behind him seemed to be;
But cliffs and darkling ocean did uprear
Behind his hand, and meadows fair to see.

He bent him down and drew the Deep more near.
He bent him lower, and along the ground
His fingers played as though it water were.

But the clear drops, to opals large and round
Changing within his hands, in many a ring
Were spilled again to earth with tuneful sound.

Then to the nearest cliff with easy swing
38

O' the loins—as in sheer pride—so light he rose
His body seemed to me a weightless thing.

But in his eyes was ever the repose
Of sleeping, and yet living, jewel-spheres.
He sat, and spoke a master-word to those

Old days we think long buried in the years,
And they returned, with saddened glory great:
Which raised his heart to laughter and to tears.

Dreamingly he had part in all men's fate,
As in his limbs he felt his vital force.
He knew no far or near, no small or great.

All life he shared in its tremendous course:
When Earth deep down grew cold with secret pang,
Darkness thronged outward from its central source,

Or night thrust forth the tepid airs that hang
On tree-tops—he rejoiced so drunkenly
That like a lion over cliffs he sprang.

·   ·   ·   ·   ·

Our soul's a Cherub and of lordly birth—
Dwells not in us, but in some upper star
Fixes his throne and leaves us oft in dearth.

Yet deep in us his fiery motions are:
—So in the dream I seemed to understand—
And he holds converse with yon fires afar,

And lives in me as I do in my hand.

THREE LITTLE SONGS.

I.

Heard'st not thou the music's tone
As around thy house it crept?
Night was heavy, no star shone,
Yet 'twas I that there alone,
Singing soft, my vigil kept.

What my tongue could tell, I spoke:
"Thou my All, my dearest, thou!"
In the east the daylight broke,
Home my heavy way I took,
And my lips are silent now.

II.

Heavy was the sky and drear,
Lonely we and full of fear,
Far apart were pining.
But 'tis now no longer so,
Back and forth the breezes flow,
And the whole wide earth is shining
Like to glass, below.

Stars meanwhile have climbed aloft,
On our cheeks they sparkle soft,
Wise with sympathy.
Yet more glory heaven revealeth,
Till through us deep longing stealeth,-
Spell-bound in an ecstasy,
Each the breath of other feeleth.

40

III.

My mistress said: "I hold thee not,
No promise hast thou sworn.
The sons of men should not be bound,
To faith they are not born.

"Then go what way thou wilt, my friend,
Beholding many a land,
And rest thyself in many a bed,
Take many a woman's hand.

"If bitter wines no longer please,
Drink thou of malmsey then;
And if my mouth seems yet more sweet,
Come back to me agen."

THE YOUNG MAN IN THE LANDSCAPE. *Man in Landscape*

Gardeners were laying out their plants in beds
And beggars, beggars wandered everywhere
With crutches, and black patches on their eyes;
But some with harps too and with fresh-plucked
       flowers—
Ah the strong scent of the weak flowers in spring!

The naked trees left all things in full view;
There was the river and the market-town
And many children playing by the ponds.
'Twas through this landscape that he slowly went,
Feeling its power and knowing in himself
That he had part in the world's destiny.

He sought those children,—strangers though they
       were,—
Ready to bring the treasures of new life
In willing service to a foreign threshold.
He reckoned not the riches of his soul,—
The ancient paths, and all the memories
Of vanished hands and spirits now transformed—
As of more value than an idle toy.

The perfume of the flowers told him but
Of unknown Beauty,—and he softly breathed
The April air, his soul unvexed by longing:
'Twas joy enough for him that he might serve.

Ship's Cook THE SHIP'S COOK, A CAPTIVE, SINGS:

Many weary weeks divide me
From my folk,—unlucky sinner!—
Worse, howe'er my foes deride me,
Still I needs must cook their dinner.

Lovely purple-gleaming fishes,
Brought me living from the water,
Stare with failing eyes reproachful;
Gentle beasts, too, I must slaughter.

Gentle beasts, too, I must slaughter,
Fruit must peel or cut in slices,
And for those who hate and scorn me
Must compound the fiery spices.

While I work beneath the lantern,
Mid the sweet, sharp odors reeling,
Thoughts of freedom rouse within me
Mighty throbs of savage feeling!

Many weary weeks divide me
From my folk,—unlucky sinner!—
Worse, howe'er my foes deride me,
Still I needs must cook their dinner.

46

AN OLD MAN'S LONGING FOR SUMMER.

If 'twere July at last instead of March,

Nothing would stop my going for a trip;
On horse-back, in a carriage or by rail
I'd get me to a fair and hilly strip

Of country.   There'd be groves of mighty trees,—
Of elms and maples, sycamores and oaks:
How long since I have looked on such as these!

There I'd dismount, or bid with sharp command
The driver: "Stop," and wander aimless on
Into the very heart of summer-land.

I'd rest beneath such trees as in their dome
Have day and night together; not that each
Should so be blurred and spoiled as here at home,—

Where day is oft as desolate as night,
And night as lurid-lowering as the day,—
For all would there be Glory, Life and Light.

From shadow into sunset, color-fraught,
I'd walk enraptured, and the breeze that came
Would never whisper: "All of this is naught."

It darkens; from the houses in the dell
The lights gleam, and the darkness weighs me down,
Yet not of dying doth the night-wind tell.

47

Longing
for Summer

I stroll across the churchyard and I see
The flowers waving in the dim last light,
No other Presence there oppresses me.

Beneath the dusky hazel-branches near
A brooklet flows, and like a child, I hark,
But no such words as: "This is vain" I hear.

Then hastily undressing, in I spring.—
I lift my head, and lo! the moon has come
While in the current I was buffeting.

Emerging half from out the ice-cold stream,
I choose a pebble, throw it landward far,
And stand there in the moonlight's pallid beam.

Across the moon-bathed summer-land doth fall
My shadow; is it this that noddeth here
So sad behind the pillow on the wall?

—So sad and dreary, he that in the dim
First light of dawn stands crouching, while he knows
That Something lies in wait for me and him?—

—He whom the rough wind never leaves at rest
This March, nor lets him once lie down at night
In peace, his black hands folded on his breast?

.   .   .   .   .

Ah, where's July and where the summer-land?

48

LINES TO A LITTLE CHILD.

Thy pink little feet have been fashioned
To seek for the Kingdom of Sunshine:
The doors of that kingdom are open.
The air these thousands of years
On the silent tree-tops is hanging,
The inexhaustible ocean
Forever and ever abides.
By the rim of the ancient forest
Wilt thou from thy wooden bowl give
The frog to drink of thy milk?
A merry meal that! yea, almost
The stars will fall into the bowl.
By the rim of the ancient ocean
Thou soon wilt find thee a playmate,
The dolphin, friendly and good.
He'll spring on dry land at thy coming
And, if he be often away,
The ancient winds will attend thee
To quiet the rising tears.
And still in the Kingdom of Sunshine
The golden heroic old days
Forever and ever abide.
'Twas the sun with his secret might—
He fashioned thy little pink feet
To enter his timeless dominions.

THE EMPEROR OF CHINA SPEAKS:

In the very midst of all things
Here dwell I, the Son of Heaven.
And my wives, my waving forests,
All my beasts and pools unnumbered—
These the inmost wall encloseth.
Underneath, my ancestors
Lie entombèd with their weapons,
With their crowns upon their foreheads,
All and each as well beseemeth,—
So they dwell there in the vaults.
Far into the world below me
Rings the echo of my footstep.
Silent from the banks of greensward—
Verdant pillows for my feet—
Glide the well-apportioned rivers
Eastward, westward, south- and northward,
To refresh the thirsty garden—
Water my wide realm, the Earth.
First my beasts' dark eyes they mirror,
And reflect the birds' bright pinions;
Then outside, the painted cities,
Gloomy walls and tangled forests,
Faces too of many peoples.
These my nobles, dwelling round me
Like the stars,—they all are known by
Names which I myself have given,
Names according to the hour
When each one drew near to me;

And their wives I also gave them,
So that for their troops of children,—
All the noblest of the earth,—
I created form and feature,
As a gardener for his flowers.
But between the walls beyond them
Peoples dwell that are my soldiers,
Peoples too that are my farmers.
Then new walls, and after these
Yon subdued and vassal peoples,
Other folk of blood more sluggish
To the ocean, the last rampart
That surrounds my realm and me.

*Emperor
of China*

GRANDMOTHER AND GRANDSON.

"Far thy mind, thy feet alone
Enter at my door."
Say, how know'st thou that so soon?
"Child, I guess at more."

What? "How sweetly she just now
Shocked thy sweet repose."—
Strange! how like herself wert thou,
Nodding, half a-doze.

"Once." . . . Nay, her I now, in truth,
See in happy trance.
"Child, thou breathest now my youth
Back with word and glance.

"Maidenhood with glowing tide
Wells in me anew,
Till my spirit opens wide."
Yes, I feel it, too.

I'm by thee, and yet away
On some distant star:
In a waking trance I sway
Now from near to far.

"When unto thy grandfather
All my life I gave,
Thoughts did not so wildly whir
As beside my grave."

52

Grave! why speakest thou of that?
Far the grave from thee!
With thy grandson dost thou chat,
Sitting peacefully.

Clear thine eyes and full of light,
Fresh thy cheek's red hue.
"Saw'st thou not where, black as night,
Something past us flew?"

Something 'tis that like a dream
Holds my loving breast.
Strangely too this room doth seem
Sultry and oppressed.

"Feel'st thou?—Yea, 'tis bright above,
Slower throbs my heart.—
When thou kissest thy true love,
From the world apart,—

"Feel it still, and think the while,
But without dismay:
With a young, young maiden's smile
Dying here I lay."

Society SOCIETY.

Singer

Listeners, if ye be but young,
Mighty is the power of song;
It can make you sad or gay,
Swift it bears the soul away.

Stranger

Peoples live both far and near;
What I show, ye gladly hear—
Not the heart of many lands,
But, as 'twere, the play of hands.

Young Man

Much that wakens joy in me
Through the fluttering scene is weaved,
But so phantom-shadowy:
Happy—I'm as one deceived.

Poet

What a soft reflected tone
Glimmers here from guest to guest—
Each one, feeling as alone,
Feels his being in the rest.

Painter

As between the candles bright
So between the faces white
See the fluttering laughter play!

54

Stranger

Song can make one sad or gay.

Poet

Great the power of song must be—
Peoples live both far and near.

Young Man

What they say I gladly hear,
Though 'tis phantom-shadowy.

PROLOGUE TO THE BOOK "ANATOL."

Trellised gateways, box-wood hedges,
Coats of arms with gilding faded,
Sphinxes glimmering through the thicket . . .
   Now the grinding doors are opened.—
With cascades that no more trickle,
Tritons weary of their spouting,
All rococo, dusty, charming,—
'Tis Vienna in the time of
Canaletto, Seventeen-and-Sixty. . . .
   Green and brown the quiet pools are,
Set in smooth white rims of marble,
And within these nixie-mirrors
Play the fishes, gold and silver. . . .
On the turf so smoothly shaven
Lie the slender, even shadows
Of the graceful oleanders;
Branches arch to form a dome here,
Branches bending form a niche there
For the stiffly-carven couples,
Loving heroines and heroes. . . .
Triple dolphins pour their murmuring
Floods into a conch-shell basin . . .
Scent-exhaling chestnut blossoms
Whir and glimmer, downward gliding,
And are drowned within the basin. . . .
   From behind a box-wood rampart
Fiddles, clarinets are sounding . . .

"Anatol" And the notes appear to gush from
Yonder graceful cupid-figures
As they sit there on the terrace,
Fiddling, twining flower-garlands,
They themselves enwreathed in flowers
Which out-stream from marble vases:
Wall-flowers, jessamine and lilacs . . .
    On the terrace too between them
Sit the fine coquettish ladies,
And the purple Monsignori . . .
In the grass, on silken cushions
At their feet, and on the stairway
Sit the gallants and abbati . . .
Others of them lift more ladies
From the depths of perfumed litters. . . .
    Lights are breaking through the branches,
Flickering on the golden tresses,
Shining on the gay-hued cushions,
Gliding over grass and pebbles,
Gliding o'er the scaffold structure
We in haste have thrown together.
Vines that clamber upward on it
Cover all the fresh-hewn timber,
And between them, rich in color,
Flutter tapestries and carpets,
Shepherd-scenes right boldly woven
From Watteau's delicious patterns . . .
With an arbor for our stage then,
Summer sun instead of foot-lights,
We are playing here at acting,

60

Playing plays ourselves have written,
Immature and sad and tender,
Comedies of our soul's passion,
Ebb and flood of our emotions,
Ugly facts in pretty symbols,
Well-turned phrases, glowing pictures,
Hidden feeling half suggested,
Episodes of tragic meaning . . .
Some, not all, are listening to them,
Some are eating ices . . . many
Too are whispering choice gallántries . . .
　In the tepid breeze are cradled
Whitely exquisite carnations,
Like white moths that swarm and flutter,
And a lap-dog of Bologna
Barks astonished at a peacock.

FOR A SIMILAR BOOK.

Attend, attend! The present time is strange,
And strange the children of the time: Ourselves.
He that's too much enamored of the sweet
Endures us not, for bitter is our way,
And odd the entertainment we afford.
    "Set up a little stage here in the room,
    The daughter of the house would give a play!"
Think you she'll trip out as a little Muse
With loose locks and bare arms, in which will rest
A not-too-heavy tinsel-gilded lyre?
Or as a shepherdess, with a white lamb
On a blue silken cord, about her lips
A smile as sweet-insipid as the rhymes
In pastoral plays? Then up! and get you gone!
Depart, I beg you, if you look for such!
You'll not endure us; we are otherwise.
For we have made a play from out the life
We live, and mingled with our comedy
Our truth keeps ever gliding in and out
As with a cunning juggler's hollow cups—
The more you look at them, the more deceived!
We cut off little shreds of our own selves
To dress the puppets. How the inner meanings—
(On which, it may be, smiles and tears are hung
Like dew-drops on a bush with shaggy leaves)
Must shudder, when they recognize themselves
Enwoven through this play of ours, half painted,
And half still like themselves, but so estranged

62

From the great guilelessness that once they had! *Similar*
Was ever play so tangled, so confusing? *Book*
It steals us from ourselves and is not lovely
As dancing is or singing on the water,
Yet 'tis the richest in seductive art
Of all the dramas that we children know,
We children of this most unusual time.
  Why are you waiting? That's the way we are.
  But if you'd really hear what things ensue,
  Well, stay. We shall not be disturbed at you.

Mitterwurzer IN MEMORY OF THE ACTOR,
MITTERWURZER.

He went out like a candle all at once.
We wore a pallor on our faces like
The hue reflected from a lightning-flash.

He fell; and with him all the puppets fell,
Into whose veins this man had poured the blood
Of his own being; silently they died,
And where he lay, a heap of corpses lay,
Strewn in disorder: here a toper's knee
Pressing a king's eye, yonder Don Philippe
With Caliban as nightmare on his neck,
Dead every one.

At last we knew him who was lost to us:
The conjurer, the mighty, mighty juggler!
And from our houses then we sallied forth
And all began to speak of who he was
Ah, but who was he, and who was he not?

From one mask he would creep into another,
Spring from the father's body to the son's,
And, like to garments, change the forms he wore
With swords, which he could swing about so fast
That no one saw the glitter of their blades,
He cut himself in pieces: This one was
Perhaps Iago, and the other half
Would take the part of some sweet fool or dreamer.
For his whole body was a magic veil,

64

Within the folds of which were dwelling all things: *Mitterwurze*
He could fetch beasts from out that self of his:
A lion, a sheep, a devil of stupidness,
And one of horror, this and yonder man,
And you and me. A sort of inward fate
Set his whole body glowing through and through,
Like coals it glowed, and he dwelt in the midst
And looked on us, who only live in houses,
With the impenetrable alien look
Of the salamander, he that lives in fire.

He was a savage king. About his hips
He carried like a string of colored shells
The truth and lies of all us other folk.
In those deep eyes of his were glassed our dreams,
That flew across, as flocks of shy wild birds
Are imaged in the mirror of a lake.

Here he would come, even to this very spot
Where I now stand, and as in Triton's horn
The clamor of the ocean is contained,
So were in him the voices of all life:
He became tall. The whole wood now he was,
He was the country that the roads ran through.
With eyes like children's we would sit and gaze
In wonder up at him, as from the slope
Of a gigantic mountain; in his mouth
There was a gulf, wherein the ocean surged.

For there was in him something that would open
Many a door and fly through many a room:

65

Mitterwurzer   The force of Life was in him, this it was.
And over him the force of Death prevailed!
For Death blew out the eyes whose inmost core
Was covered with mysterious hieroglyphs,
It strangled in the throat a thousand voices,
And killed the body which through every limb
Was laden down with life as yet unborn.

'Twas here he stood.   When will his like stand
        here?—
A spirit peopling all the labyrinth
Of the human breast with forms it comprehends,
And opening it anew to fearsome joys.
Those which he gave we can no longer keep,
We hear his name and stare with vague affright
Down the abyss that swallowed them from sight.

66

ON THE DEATH OF THE ACTOR, HERMANN MULLER.

Müller

This house and we are servants to an art
Which turns each grief to some refreshing draught,
And gives even Death a relish.

And he whom we would call before our souls,
He was so strong! his body so endowed
With power of change that, as it seemed, no net
Was able to contain him! What a being!
He made himself transparent, let the whites
Of his eye betray the utmost secrecies
That slumbered there within him, and he breathed
The spirits of imaginary creatures
Into himself like smoke and sent them through
His pores again into the light of day.
He would transform himself, and out would well
Strange beings, hardly human, but so living—
The eye said yes to them, although before
It ne'er had seen the like: one little twinkle,
One fetch of the breath would prove that such
        things were,
And still might steam from out our mother earth.
And men! Ah, close your eye-lids and think back!
Now splendid bodies, where one last least spark
Of soul gleams but in the corner of an eye,
Now souls that build as body round themselves,
Only to serve them, a transparent shrine:
Commonplace men, and gloomy men, and kings,

67

Müller Men that could make you laugh, could make you
            shudder—
He would transform himself, and there they stood.

But when the play was quenched and when the
            curtain
Silently like a painted eye-lid fell
Across the cavern of dead wizardry,
And he himself went forth, a stage was then
Opened before him in such wise it seemed
A staring, ever sleepless eye, a stage
On which no pitying curtain ever sinks:
The terror-striking stage, Reality.
There all his arts of transformation fell
Away from him, and his poor spirit went
Unveiled and could but see through childish eyes.
There he, unknowing how it came about,
Was caught in an inexorable play;
Each step entangled worse than that before,
And each inanimate thing was cruel toward him:
The countenance of night conspired as well,
The wind conspired, the gentle wind of spring,
And all *against* him! Not for common souls,
For delicate souls it is that darkling Fate
Sets nooses of this sort. Then came a day:
He raised himself, and his tormented eye
Was flooded with foreboding and with dream,
And with firm grasp, like to a heavy cloak
He threw life off from him and did not heed
68

More than the dust upon his mantle's hem   *Müller*
The forms that now were crumbled into naught.

Think only thus of him.   Let reverent music
Call him before you, dimly guess his fate,
And let me cease, for I have reached the bounds
Where awe shatters the word within my mouth.

Böcklin FOR A COMMEMORATION ON THE
DEATH OF ARNOLD BÖCKLIN.

[*During the last bars of the music the speaker of the
prologue advances, his torch-bearers following. The
speaker is a youth dressed in the Venetian style, all
in black, as a mourner.*]

Music, be silent! Now the scene is mine,
And now will I lament, as well I should!
In these my years the sap of youth runs strong
Within, and he whose statue looks on me
Was to my spirit a belovèd friend.
And of such favor was I sore in need,
For gloom oppresses much in these my years;
And as the swan, a happy swimming creature,
Kisses its nourishment from out the white
And dripping hands of naiads, even so
I bent me in dark hours above *his* hands
To take the food my soul would have: deep dream.
Shall I adorn thy statue but with flowers?
Thou did'st adorn the image of the world
For me, and did'st enhance with such a glow
The loveliness of every blossoming spray,
I threw myself all drunken on the earth,
I cried exultant, feeling how for me
Shining-limbed Nature let her robe sink down!
Harken to me, my friend! I will not bid
Heralds go out and trumpet forth thy name
To the four winds, as though a king were dead:
70

A king leaves to his heir his royal crown,   *Bocklin*
And to a tomb the echo of his name,
But thou wert a magician of such might
That, though thy visible self is gone, there lurks
An oh I know not what of thee here and there,—
Which, dark of eye, with strange still-living power
Lifts itself to the bank from out the flood
Of night—or stretches out a hairy ear
Listening behind the ivy.
                              So I'll not
Believe that I am anywhere alone,
Where there are trees or flowers, where even are
But silence-keeping rocks and tiny clouds
Beneath the heavens: how easily a Something,
A more transparent shape than Ariel was,
Might flit away behind me! For I know
That there was knit a secret bond 'twixt thee
And many a creature, yea, the field in spring—
Behold! it laughed on thee as might a woman
On him to whom by night she gave herself.

I purposed to lament you, and my mouth
Swells with a flood of glad and drunken speech:
Thus it befits I stand no longer here.
I'll strike my thyrsus on the ground three times
And fill this tent-like space with forms of dream.
These will I so o'erburden with the weight
Of sadness, they shall stagger as they go,
At which whoever sees must weep and feel
With how great sorrow is enmingled all

Böcklin That we may do.

Let now a play reveal
The mirror of yon dark and anxious hour,
And do ye learn from shadowy lips what prize
Is the great master's melancholy dower!

IDYLL

AFTER AN OLD VASE PAINTING: A CENTAUR ON THE
BANK OF A RIVER CARRYING A WOUNDED WOMAN.

[*The scene is in the style of a painting by Böcklin.
An open village smithy. Behind the house in the
background, a stream. The smith is at his work, his
wife leans idly in the doorway which leads from the
smithy into the house. On the floor a little fair-
haired child is playing with a tame crab. In a niche
is a skin of wine, some fresh figs, and slices of
melon.*]

THE SMITH

Where do your musing thoughts betake themselves,
While silently, with hostile air almost
And lightly twitching lips, you watch my toil?

THE WOMAN

I often sat in a garden, blossom-white,
Turning my gaze upon my father's work,
The comely potter's craft, as on the disk,
That, humming, whirled, a noble form would rise
In quiet growth like to a tender flower,
With the cool glint of ivory. Then to this
He set a handle with acanthus leaves.
An olive- or acanthus-garland too,
Dark-red, went round to ornament the rim.
The body he enlivened with a row

75

Idyll O' the Hours, the Hovering Life-outpouring Ones.
He wrought the wondrous form of Phædra, faint
With longing, stretched upon her royal couch;
And Eros fluttering above her there,
Eros that filled her limbs with sweetest pain.
He loved to decorate a mighty jug
With bacchic revelry, where purple must
Would spurt beneath the mænad's naked foot,
And all the air was filled with tossing hair
And waving of the thyrsus, held aloft.
On mortuary urns Persephone
Was pictured, with her reddened soulless eyes,
And poppies, flowers of forgetfulness,
Twined in her sacred tresses, while she trod
The life-oblivious fields of asphodel.
I'd never end, were I to tell of all
The godlike beings, in whose lovely life,
—Living a second time what there I saw,—
In all their fear and hatred and desire
And strange adventures of whatever sort—
I also had my share, though but a child.
The breath of their emotions, half divined,
Touched on the deepest harp-strings of my soul,
So that at times methought that I in sleep
Had wandered through the dark-hid mysteries
Of Joy and Grief with open, conscious eye.
Hence, though I'm now returned to sunlight, still
My thoughts are mindful of that other life,
Making of me a stranger, one shut out
Here in the world of healthful living air.
76

THE SMITH   *Idyll*

Overmuch idleness confused, methinks,
The sense of being in the fanciful
And dream-delighted child.   There lacked besides
The high respect which wisely separates
Things fit for gods alone from those which gods
Allow to mortals.   This did Semele,
Her mad wish granted, feel as she expired.
Learn to revere your husband's handicraft,—
Born of the entrails of all-mothering Earth—
Which, having first subdued the hundred-armed
Unfettered flame, does deft and mighty work.

THE WOMAN

To watch the flame, that lure is ever new,—
The changeful, with its hot bewildering breath.

THE SMITH

Rather rejoice to gaze upon the work!
The weapons, look! the sacred plough's hard blade,
This axe that shapes the tree trunks for our house.
So does the smith make that which makes all else.
Where pungent upturned furrows drink the seeds
And yellow wheat against the sickle flows,
Where through still branches toward the startled
       deer
The arrow whirs and strikes into its neck,
Where the hard horse-hoofs, thudding, spurn the
       dust

Idyll And rapid wheels roll between town and town,
And where with ringing blade the strife of men
Reveals the manhood that should live in song:
Thus I work on and hold the world thus bound
With tokens of my work, because 'tis good.

[Pause.]

THE WOMAN

I see a centaur coming, young he is,
A beauteous god, methinks, though half a beast;
He leaves the wood and trots along the bank.

THE CENTAUR

[*He has in his hand a spear, which he holds out
toward the smith.*]
May my dull weapon here find remedy
And a new point to suit its weight? Reply!

THE SMITH

I've seen your like before, but never you.

THE CENTAUR

For the first time now has my course been lured
Into your village by the need you know of.

THE SMITH

'Twill soon be satisfied. Do you, meanwhile,
If you would win this woman's gratitude,

Tell of the wonders you'll have seen, whereof   *Idyll*
No tidings come here, if no wanderer comes.

THE WOMAN

I'll bring you first the wine-skin: it is filled
With cool sharp cider; nothing else have we.

[*She has poured the wine from the skin into an
earthen drinking-cup, which he slowly empties.*]

Next time you'll drink—right far from here per-
            chance—
A warmer liquor from a better cup
Filled by a woman fairer than am I.

THE CENTAUR

I went not on the common streets, I shunned
The thronging bustle of the landing-place,
Where one may glean gay news from sailor-folk.
The barren heath I chose as path by day,
Rousing flamingoes only or black bulls;
And stamped the heather into scent by night,
Roaming beneath the hyacinthine dusk.
Once as I wandered by a sacred grove,
Suddenly in some whim of wilful joy,
Out of a troop of naiads one came forth
And joined me for a space, whom then I lost
Again to a young satyr by the road
Blowing his syrinx-pipes enticingly.

THE WOMAN

Unspeakably sweet this freedom seems to me.

79

Idyll THE SMITH

The wood-born creatures know not shame or faith,
Which learn to long for and to guard the house.

THE WOMAN

Say, did you chance to hear the flute of Pan?

THE CENTAUR

In a deep valley it was granted me.
Borne from the cliff's edge on the sultry wind
Of evening, eerie notes came floating down,
Deeply disturbing as the stress combined
Of all deep things that tremble through the soul;
It was as if my self was whirled away
Through myriad-shifting moods of drunkenness.

THE SMITH

Forbidden things leave rather undescribed!

THE WOMAN

Nay, let him!—What more sweetly stirs the soul?

THE SMITH

'Tis life matures the pulsing of the heart,
As ripened fruit will gladly leave the twig.
And to no other shuddering are we born
Than fate breathes o'er the surface of our life.

THE CENTAUR *Idyll*

Would you know nothing of the wondrous art
Which the gods use, O man beneath your race,
Of mounting in the storm to other times;
As dolphin splashing in the primal wet,
Or circling through the air with eagle-joy?
Friend, you know little of the world, methinks.

THE SMITH

I know the whole, who know my proper sphere,
I shun the measureless, desiring not
To cup the fleeting wave with hollow hand.
Know first the brook that rocked your cradle; know
Yon tree, with fruit the sun makes ripe for you,
Whence tepid perfume-laden shadows pour;
The cool green grass,—you trod it as a child.
Your sire walked there, with gently chilling blood;
Your sweetheart too, beneath whose step welled up
The scented violets, nestling at her feet.
Know too the house where you shall live and die;
Then reverently know yourself, your work.
In this there will be more than you can grasp.—
I'll not detain the wanderer, except
For a last polishing. The file's not here;
I'll find it, so that all may be complete.

> [*He goes into the house.*]

THE WOMAN

Your way will never lead you here again;
And, trampling through the hyacinthine night,

81

Idyll Enraptured, you will soon, I fear, forget
Me, who, I fear, will not forget so soon.

THE CENTAUR

You're wrong. I were accurst in leaving you,
As though behind me rumbling gates should close
Upon the perfumed garden of all love.
But 'tis my meaning you should come with me;
I'd take along such rapture as today's,—
Joy that Queen Aphrodite ne'er poured out,
Who quickens all the ocean and the plain.

THE WOMAN

How could I leave my husband, house and child?

THE CENTAUR

How should you grieve for what you'll soon forget?

THE WOMAN

He's coming back; the dream is soon dissolved!

THE CENTAUR

Never, while joy and way are still to choose.
Twine your firm fingers in my mane and cling,
Resting upon my back, to neck and arms!

[*She swings herself up on his back, and he dashes
down to the river with shrill cries, the child becomes
frightened and breaks into pitiful weeping. The*

smith steps out of the house. Just then the centaur *Idyll*
plunges into the rushing waters of the stream. His
bronze breast and the figure of the woman stand out
sharply against the surface which is gilded by the
sunset. The smith sees them; with the spear of the
centaur in his hand he runs down to the bank and,
bending far forward, casts the spear. It strikes and
remains for a moment fixed with quivering shaft in
the back of the woman, till with a piercing cry she
looses the mane of the centaur and with arms out-
spread falls backward into the water. The centaur
catches her, dying, in his arms and, lifting her on
high, bears her down the river while he swims
toward the opposite bank.]